SEP. 0 8 2003

Science Matters! | Volume 4

Rocks and soils

A brief history

TODAY... 1830 In Britain Charles Lyell states that the Earth is hundreds of millions of years old (it is now known to be 4.6 billion years old)... 1822 Friedrich Mohs of Germany makes up a scale for the hardness of materials. It goes from 1 to 10... 1797 Sir James Hall, in Britain, proves that volcanic lava cools to make rock... 1785 In Britain James Hutton shows that the rocks of the past were formed in the same way as rocks are forming today. As a result, he believes the Earth is extremely old. Hutton becomes known as the father of geology... 1779 Horace de Saussure, in France, invents the word geology for the study of the Earth's rocks... 1776 James Keir, in Britain, suggests that many rocks are produced from volcanoes... 1774 Abraham Werner, in Germany, works out a way to compare and sort out the minerals that make up the world's rocks. He uses properties such as color and hardness. He states that rocks are made of layers, with the oldest at the bottom and the youngest at the top. Before this everyone thought that all rocks were the same age. He also says that some rocks were formed from sand and mud settling out of the seabed... 1650 Archbishop Usher, in Britain, uses the Bible to figure out that the Earth and its rocks were all formed in 4004 B.C. ...

Dr. Brian Knapp

Word list

These are some science words that you should look out for as you go through the book. They are shown using CAPITAL letters.

ABSORB
To soak up.

ACID
A liquid that destroys many materials, including rocks. Vinegar is a very weak acid. Rainwater is an extremely weak acid.

BRICK
A block of clay that has been baked in an oven (a kiln).

CEMENT
A powder, made partly from baked limestone, that is added to water to make a kind of glue for holding rocks together.

CHALK
A soft, white, and very pure kind of limestone rock. It absorbs water easily.

CLAY
A soft, sticky material made of pieces of rock too fine to see without a microscope.

CONCRETE
A mixture of cement, sand, and stones.

GRANITE
A hard white or gray rock speckled with black.

LAVA
The name for both the liquid that is erupted from a volcano and the cooled rock. Lava rock has tiny bubbles in it.

LIMESTONE
A hard gray or cream-colored rock made of the remains of the shells of ancient sea creatures.

LOAM
A soil that is an even mixture of all sizes of particles from sand to clay.

MARBLE
A type of limestone rock baked underground. It is often white with colored veins running through it.

MUD
The name for fine material in water.

PEBBLES
Rounded stones.

QUARRY
A place where building stone is dug up.

ROCK
A hard material made up of small pieces that have been melted or squashed together while deep underground.

SAND
Small pieces of rock, like the material found on a beach.

SANDSTONE
A rock made from cemented sand grains.

SLATE
A rock made of clay that breaks up into thin sheets.

SOIL
A mixture of stones, sand, clay, and rotting plant and animal material.

STONE
A small piece of rock or a type of rock that is useful for building.

SUBSOIL
The layer of soil that lies between the surface layer and the rock below.

TOPSOIL
The top layer of a soil. It is darker than the layer below.

Contents

Rock and soil

The Earth's surface is made of rocks, but they are mostly covered up with soils. You can find bare rocks if you know where to look.

▼ (Picture 1) Soil is a thin layer on top of rock.

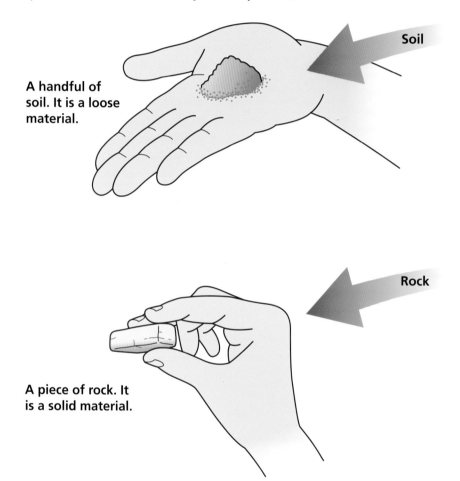

A handful of soil. It is a loose material.

Soil

A piece of rock. It is a solid material.

Rock

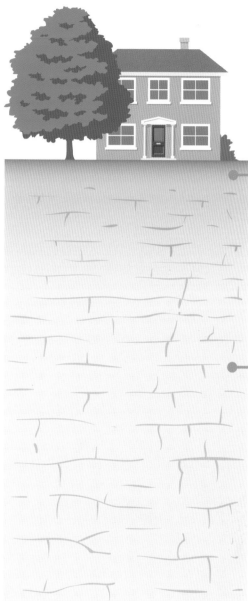

Most of us rarely see large amounts of **ROCK**. That is very strange because the whole of the Earth's surface is made of rock. However, in most places the rocks are covered up by soil (Picture 1), so you have to know where to look to find them.

Rocks can be seen in seaside cliffs and in quarries (Picture 2). When you look into a **QUARRY**, you can see that we live on a world of solid rock.

Rock and soil

Between us and rock there is a layer of soft, loose material. It is called **SOIL**. A soil is made of tiny pieces. Soil covers the rock. It is only a meter or so thick.

▼ (Picture 2) This is a quarry in Cornwall, England. So much rock has been taken away that there is now a very deep hole.

At the top of the picture you can see houses. They help you see how deep the quarry is.

Summary

• Rock is solid material, such as seen in a quarry.

• Soil lies on top of rock.

⚠ Never go alone near a quarry or a rocky cliff.

Rocks from volcanoes

Many rocks begin in the fiery fountains of volcanoes.

How do rocks come to make up the surface of the Earth? Many of them come from erupting volcanoes.

Liquid rock

Deep underground the rock is liquid. From time to time it bursts to the surface and forms a volcanic eruption (Pictures 1 and 2).

Lava

The runny material spewing from a volcano is called **LAVA**. It is red-hot and flows over the land like a river (Picture 2). As it cools, however, it loses its red color and turns black. The cooled material is hard rock (Picture 3).

▼ **(Picture 1) This is a volcano erupting lava.**

A volcano forms where the liquid rock pours out over the Earth's surface in lava flows.

▶ (Picture 3) This is a piece of cooled lava.

▲ (Picture 2) This is how a volcano works: Liquid rock in a chamber deep below the surface bursts up through cracks and erupts at the surface.

Chamber of liquid rock.

▼ (Picture 4) Underground the liquid rock cools slowly to make granite rock.

Granite is white or gray with specks of other colors in it.

Granite

When the eruption is over, hard black rock lies all around the volcano. The liquid rock still underground begins to cool too. In time it forms a rock called **GRANITE**.

Granite is a white or gray rock with specks of other colors in it (Picture 4).

Summary
- Volcanic rocks include lava and granite. All volcanic rocks are made from liquid rock.
- Granite is a hard gray speckled rock.

Hard and soft rocks

Some rocks are much harder than others. That affects how they are used.

There are many different kinds of rock. Some rocks come from volcanoes. Other rocks are made in different ways. They all vary in hardness. Only the really hard ones are useful in building.

Hard or soft?

A rock is made of small grains. The hardness of a rock depends on what these grains are made of and what kind of natural glue holds them together.

Rocks made of **MUD** (**CLAY** and water) have no "glue" holding them together. They are nearly all soft (Picture 1).

Rocks made from **SAND** (Picture 2) or shells (Picture 3) are glued together by natural cements. If the **CEMENT** is hard,

▲ (Picture 2) A rock made from sand feels like the sand you find on a beach—and it is often the same color, too. You can see the sand grains easily. The grains feel rough to the touch. This type of rock is called SANDSTONE.

◀ (Picture 1) Mud squashes into a soft rock we call mudstone or shale. Mud is so fine we can't see the grains. This kind of rock feels smooth to the touch.

the rock is hard; but if the cement is soft, the rock is soft.

Rocks that have been baked when deep underground are always very hard (Picture 4). **MARBLE** is one of these rocks.

▲ (Picture 3) LIMESTONE is made from seashells. It can be white or gray. CHALK is a soft, very white form of limestone.

▼ (Picture 4) Marble has been baked into a very hard rock while deep underground.

Testing for rock hardness

It is not easy to tell which rocks are hard and which are soft just by looking at them. To find out whether one rock is harder than another, we can rub rocks gently together and see which one rubs away (Picture 5). The one that rubs away is the softer rock.

▼ (Picture 5) Testing for hardness by rubbing two samples together.

Summary
- Hard rocks are useful as building materials.
- Soft rocks are rarely used for building.
- Rock hardness can be tested by rubbing.

Rocks shape the land

The shape of the land is often similar to the pattern of the hard and soft rocks below it.

Rocks lie beneath everything. So if you look around from, say, a hilltop, the shape of the land is often made by the shape of the rocks below.

Flat rocks

Rocks that lie in flat sheets make tablelands (Picture 1). If they are cut into by rivers or the sea, then the hard layers of rock make tall cliffs, while the soft layers of rock form more gentle slopes.

Sloping rocks

When sloping rocks lie underground, the pattern of hills and valleys tells us where the hard and softer bands of rock are found (Picture 2). The hills match the bands of hard rock, while the valleys match the bands of soft rock.

▼ (Picture 1) This flat-topped land in a desert is called a tableland. Beneath it there are layers of flat rock. Notice how the cliff is made of just one kind of rock. It is a very hard rock.

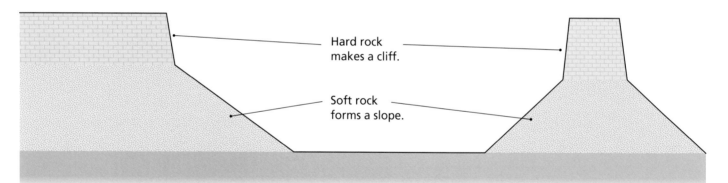

Hard rock makes a cliff.

Soft rock forms a slope.

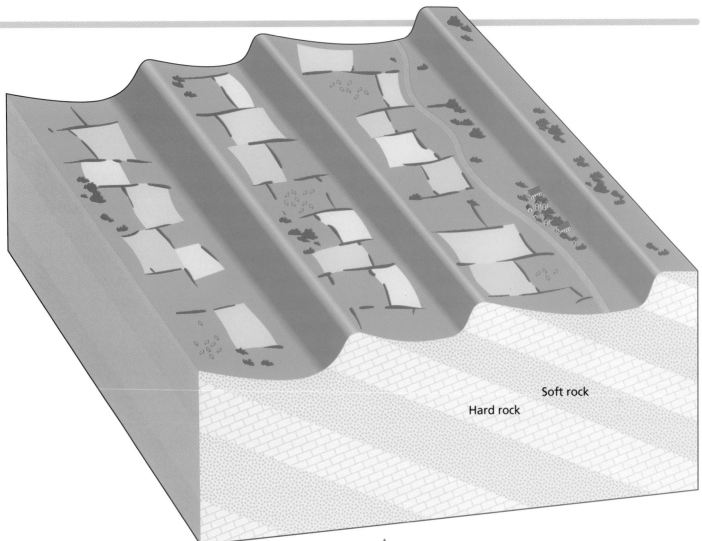

(Picture 2) This picture shows what the rocks might be like under a land of hills and valleys. Notice that the flatter parts are used for farming because that is where soils are thickest.

Soft rock

Hard rock

Old volcanoes

The original pipe that fed lava during a volcanic eruption fills up with lava as the volcano goes silent. This lava is hard and often remains as a pillar of rock (Picture 3).

▶ **(Picture 3)** In this picture a church has been built on the top of an old volcanic pipe. The rest of the volcano has been worn away.

Summary

- Hard rocks form hills.
- Soft rocks form valleys.
- Flat sheets of rock make tablelands.

Rocks that soak up water

LIMESTONE rocks soak up water quickly. Most other rocks are waterproof.

Over time water destroys all rocks, turning them into soil. If water cannot get inside a rock, then the rock is destroyed very slowly. However, some rocks soak up or **ABSORB** water. When they do so, they can be destroyed very quickly.

Why rocks soak up water

Water will flow into any small crack and hole in a rock. However, some rocks—volcanic rocks like granite and baked rocks like **SLATE** and marble—have no gaps and so are waterproof (Picture 1A). But other rocks have just the right-sized holes for water to flow into. Water soaks into these rocks just as it does into a sponge.

The rocks that soak up water most easily are **CHALK** and **SANDSTONE** (Picture 1B).

▼ **(Picture 1)** A simple test will show which rocks are waterproof, and which soak up water. Add small drops of water to the rock, and see if the water soaks in.

A

When water is slowly dripped onto a block of slate, the water runs off. That is why slate is used as a roofing stone.

B

When water is added a drop at a time to a block of chalk, it soaks in.

Why rocks crumble

When rocks soak up water and then freeze, they crumble easily. You can see why this happens by putting a bag of wetted chalk in a freezer and letting it freeze (Picture 2). The water expands as it freezes, breaking the chalk apart.

Why rocks get eaten away

Rain contains chemicals (called **ACIDS**) that can slowly eat away some rocks. Acids work most quickly on soft rocks like chalk and limestone. Some sandstones are also held together by a natural cement. When acid is added, this cement is eaten away. Over time limestone will completely disappear, while sandstone will fall apart. You can see this working by putting a block of chalk in some vinegar, which is also an acid (Picture 3).

◀ **(Picture 2)** Soak a small piece of chalk in water, and then put it in a plastic bag in a freezer. Take the sample out of the bag, and allow it to thaw. The freezing water cracks the rock apart. When the chalk is allowed to thaw, the rock crumbles.

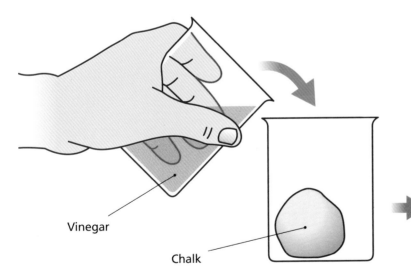

Vinegar

Chalk

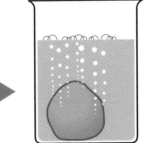

▲ **(Picture 3)** Take a small piece of chalk, and put it in a glass with some vinegar. The vinegar is an acid, so the chalk will slowly disappear.

Summary

- Chalks and sandstones can absorb water.
- Wet rocks that have soaked up water crumble if they freeze.
- Chalks and limestones can be eaten away by acids.

How rocks are used

Hard rocks have many uses. They are used to make all types of buildings and even to make roads.

Blocks of rock that are cut from a quarry are called **STONE**. People have found hard stone to be a very useful material for thousands of years (Picture 1). It is still used in huge amounts even today.

In the past the only long-lasting building material was stone. All important buildings, such as cathedrals, palaces, and temples, were made of stone. Stone was also used by wealthy people for their houses.

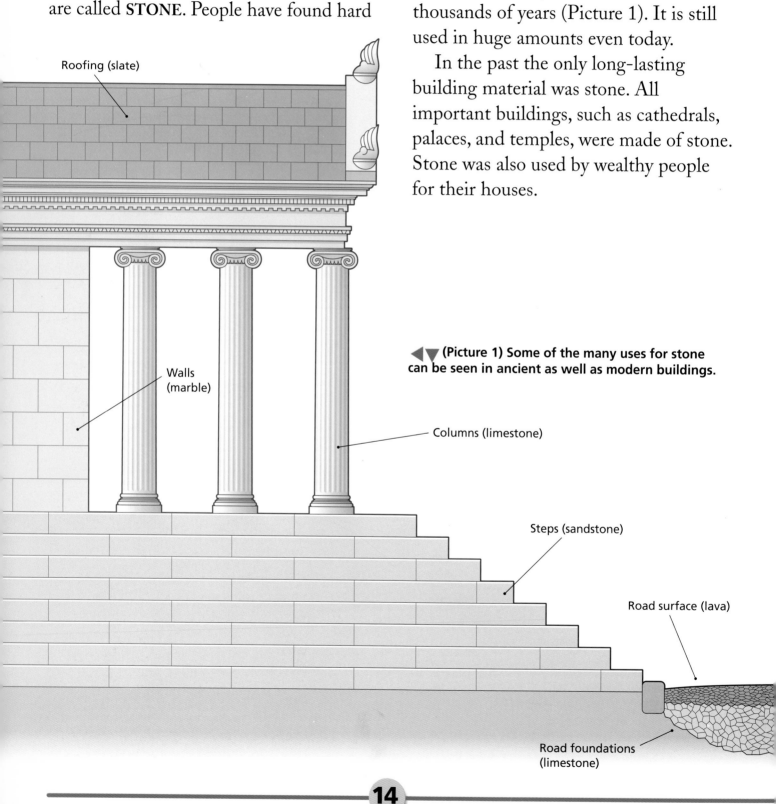

Roofing (slate)

Walls (marble)

(Picture 1) Some of the many uses for stone can be seen in ancient as well as modern buildings.

Columns (limestone)

Steps (sandstone)

Road surface (lava)

Road foundations (limestone)

Building stone

Some stone, such as **LIMESTONE**, can be cut into in large blocks. This makes it especially useful for building (Pictures 2 and 3).

Some stone, such as slate, breaks up into sheets. They can be used as thin slabs to make roofs.

Some stone, such as granite and marble, looks very attractive when it is polished. These types of stone are often used for decoration as statues, floors or the outsides of buildings.

▼ (Picture 3) Any hard stone can be used to make walls. This is limestone. This type of wall is called a dry stone wall because no cement has been used between the blocks.

▲ (Picture 2) This building uses limestone blocks for the walls.

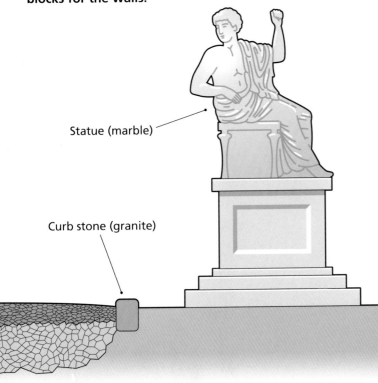

Statue (marble)

Curb stone (granite)

Road stone

Roads have to take the weight of trucks and be hard-wearing. They are mainly made of hard stone.

For this purpose the stone is quarried using explosives, then it is crushed up. Large pieces are used as foundations for roads. Small pieces are covered in tar and used to make the road surface.

Summary
- Only hard rock is useful for building.
- Rocks that can be cut into shapes are used for building.
- Pieces of hard rock are used for roads.

Artificial rocks

The main artificial rocks are bricks and concrete. They are easier to use for building than natural stone.

Building stone is expensive to quarry and difficult to cut into the right shapes. That is why for thousands of years people have made artificial rocks. We use them for building materials. The most common are **BRICKS** and **CONCRETE**.

Bricks

Bricks begin as **CLAY**. Clay is a soft, sticky material when wet. But as it dries, it begins to get very hard. The simplest bricks are wet clay shaped into a block and allowed to dry in the sun.

These kinds of bricks are only suited to very dry places because rain will make them wet, and they will fall apart. But if the clay is baked, then it becomes hard, strong, and waterproof. This makes true bricks.

Bricks are used mainly for walls (Picture 1). They are also sometimes used for pavements (Picture 2).

Concrete

Concrete is a mixture of sand, cement, and stones. The stones give the concrete its strength, and the cement binds them together.

The advantage of concrete is that it can be poured into molds and made to take on any shape (Pictures 2 and 3).

◀ (Picture 1) Bricks are cemented into place in an overlapping pattern to make the wall strong.

▲ (Picture 2) Bricks are used for low buildings and for paving the footpath here, but they cannot support the weight of a tall building. All of the tall buildings in the background are made of concrete built around a metal frame.

▶ (Picture 3) Concrete can be poured into shapes or used for paving slabs and curbstones. All these uses are seen in the Sydney Opera House, shown here.

Summary

- Artificial rocks include bricks and concrete.
- Artificial rocks are used because they are easier to work with than natural stone.

Pebbles, sand, and clay

8

As rocks roll down river beds, they get broken down into smaller pieces. We call these pieces pebbles, sand, and clay.

The bed of most rivers is covered with small pieces of rock that have been worn into rounded shapes.

Pebbles, sand, and clay

The large pieces of rounded rock we call **PEBBLES**. They are big enough for us to see that they are made of rock.

Sand is too small for you to see that it is made of rock (Picture 1). But when rubbed between the fingers, it feels rough, or gritty.

The finest pieces of rock are called mud or clay. You cannot see these grains because they are too small. They are what make water look muddy.

How rock is made smaller

All pebbles, sand, and clay start out as rock. The force of water in rivers and streams carries rocks along, bouncing them along the riverbed (Picture 2A) so they crash into one another and the riverbed. Each crash breaks off small chips from the corners or edges.

In time the rocks get smaller and more rounded (Picture 2B). The chippings may make sand, while the chipped rock becomes a pebble.

Bouncing, crashing, and chipping continue, so that rocks become smaller as they get farther down the river.

If you look in the banks of a river, you can often see all three types of material together (Picture 3).

◀ (Picture 1) Here you can see pebbles (bottom left) and sand (top right).

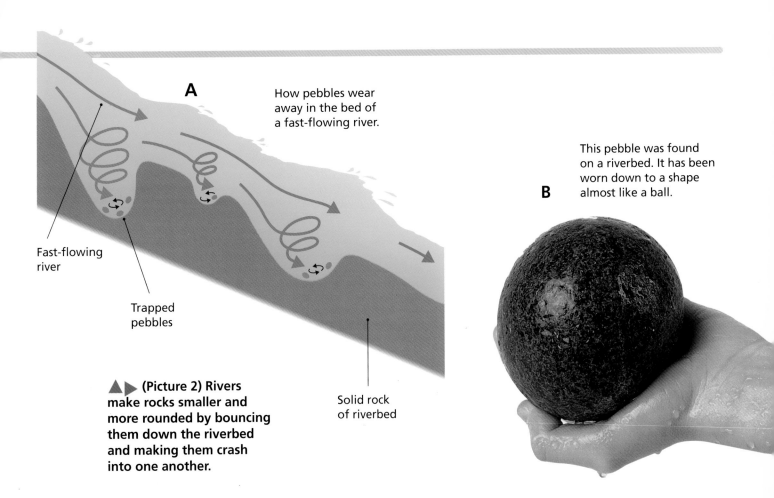

A How pebbles wear away in the bed of a fast-flowing river.

Fast-flowing river

Trapped pebbles

Solid rock of riverbed

▲▶ (Picture 2) Rivers make rocks smaller and more rounded by bouncing them down the riverbed and making them crash into one another.

B This pebble was found on a riverbed. It has been worn down to a shape almost like a ball.

▲ (Picture 3) Pebbles, sand, and clay occur in this riverbank. If you were to take a sample and shake it in water, you would see the three types separate.

Summary

- Pebbles, sand, and clay are different sizes of rock worn down by rivers.
- As rock becomes worn down, it becomes more rounded.

Soils from rocks

Soils are made from rocks, but they are not hard like rocks.

Rocks are tough materials. But as they break down into smaller pieces, they make a thin layer on the surface. It is called a soil.

What is a soil made of?

A soil is a mixture of materials. It contains mostly fine pieces of rock such as clay and sand. It may also contain a few stones.

But if this was all there was, it would not be a soil. A soil also contains plant and animal remains. So a soil is a mixture of rock and plant and animal remains.

Soil layers

Soils form in layers (Picture 1).

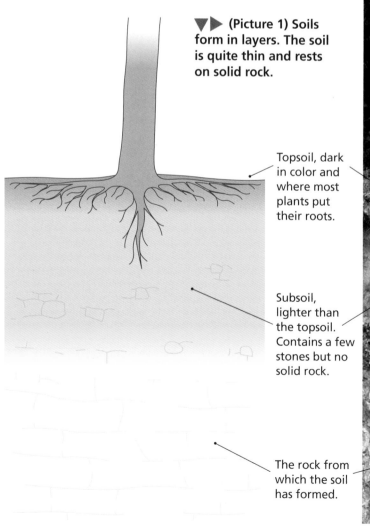

▼▶ (Picture 1) Soils form in layers. The soil is quite thin and rests on solid rock.

Topsoil, dark in color and where most plants put their roots.

Subsoil, lighter than the topsoil. Contains a few stones but no solid rock.

The rock from which the soil has formed.

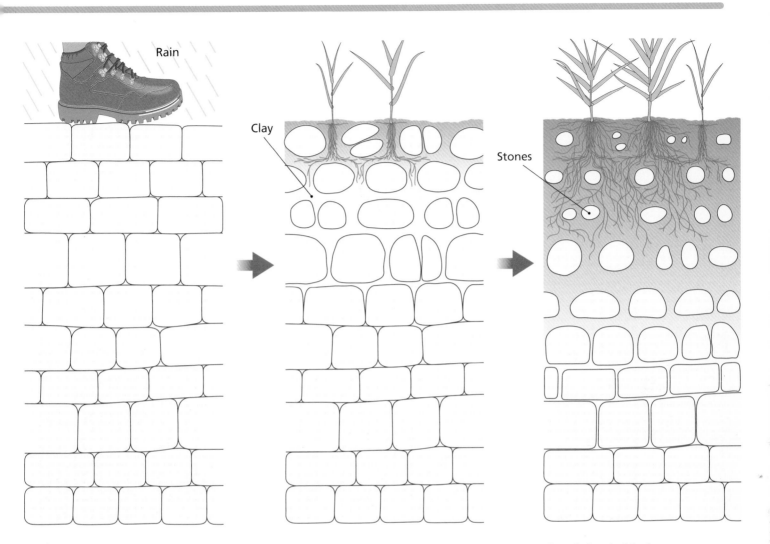

▲ (Picture 2) Rain falling onto rock soaks in and begins to destroy it. That leaves sand and clay behind. The stones are the remains of the original rock.

The top layer of the soil is called the **TOPSOIL**. It is dark in color. Here you find clay, sand, and plant roots.

Below the topsoil is a lighter layer. It is the **SUBSOIL**. Few plant roots are found here. The subsoil rests on the solid rock.

How soils form

Soils form as rainwater causes the rock to break up (Picture 2).

You can think of the way soil is made from rock by comparing the way brown rust forms on a nail. As the nail is attacked by the weather, it becomes soft and flaky. When rock is attacked by the weather, it too becomes soft and loose.

Rocks, like nails, contain iron, and so they also turn brown when breaking up into soils as a result of attacks by the weather.

Summary

- Soils form in layers.
- Soils form above rocks.
- Soils are produced when rocks are attacked by the weather.

Soils and water

Some soils let water pass quickly through them. They easily get dry and dusty in summer. Other soils hold the water for plants to use.

Have you ever seen countryside or school playing fields covered with water? These soils are waterlogged—they can't let the rainwater seep through fast enough.

Have you ever noticed that the grass dries out and turns brown on some parts of a playing field during the summer, while it stays green elsewhere? Soils that dry out quickly can't store enough water for plants during a drought.

To know why some soils become waterlogged and why others dry out quickly, you need to investigate the way water passes through a soil (Picture 1).

How water flows through soils

A soil is made of many tiny grains packed together (Picture 2).

If all the grains are small, they pack together very well, leaving only small gaps in between. It is hard for water to squeeze through these tiny spaces. Instead, the water seeps in and gets stuck inside. Clay soils are made of tiny grains. Clay soils easily fill up with water and become waterlogged.

If all the grains are large, the gaps between them are large, so that water easily flows through. But very little water is trapped. Sandy soils are made of large grains, and so they easily dry out.

If there is a mixture of soil grains, then there are some big gaps, which let the water flow through, but some small ones to store water, too. These are the best kinds of soils. A soil with a mixture of all kinds of sizes is known as **LOAM**.

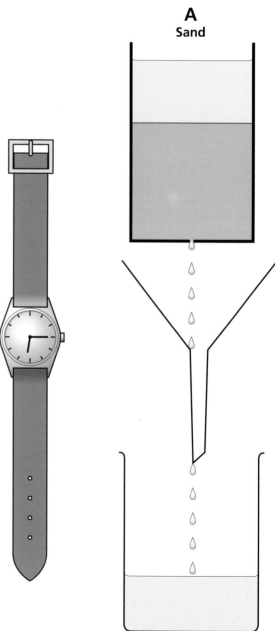

A
Sand

▼ (Picture 1) This test was set up to see how water passed through different soils.

Three pots of the same size and with the same sized drainage holes were filled with the same amounts of different soils. The same amount of water was added to each soil, and each soil was allowed to drain the water for the same amount of time. The amount of water that passed through the soil in this time showed how well the soil drained.

The results show that a sandy soil drains quickly (A), while a clay soil drains slowly (B). Neither is a good soil. What is needed is a loam soil that drains well but holds some water (C).

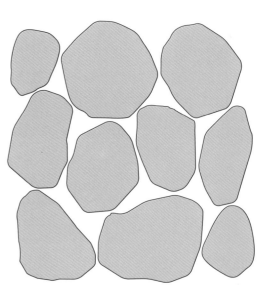

▲▼ (Picture 2) The gaps between sand grains are large. The gaps between clay grains are small.

B
Clay

C
Loam
(sand and clay mix)

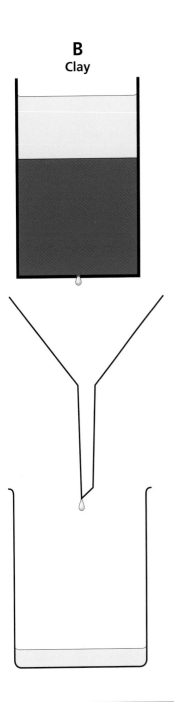

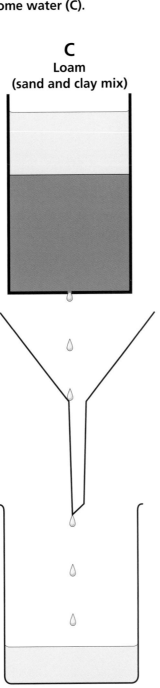

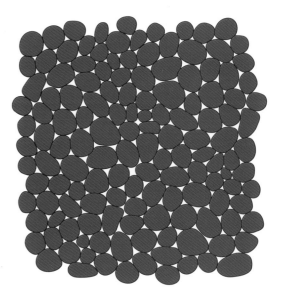

Summary

- Sandy soils do not hold water well.
- Clay soils fill up with water.
- Loam soils drain well and keep back enough water for plants.

Index

Science Matters!

Grolier Educational

First published in the United States in 2003 by Grolier Educational, Sherman Turnpike, Danbury, CT 06816

Copyright © 2003
Atlantic Europe Publishing Company Ltd.

All rights reserved. No part of this publication may be reproduced, stored in a retrieval system, or transmitted in any form or by any means—electronic, mechanical, photocopying, recording, or otherwise—without prior permission of the publisher.

This product is manufactured from sustainable managed forests. For every tree cut down at least one more is planted.

Author
Brian Knapp, BSc, PhD

Educational Consultant
Peter Riley, BSc, C Biol, MI Biol, PGCE

Art Director
Duncan McCrae, BSc

Senior Designer
Adele Humphries, BA, PGCE

Editor
Lisa Magloff, BA

Illustrations
David Woodroffe

Designed and produced by
Earthscape Editions

Reproduced in Malaysia by
Global Color

Printed in Hong Kong by
Wing King Tong Company Ltd

Picture credits
All photographs are from the Earthscape Editions photolibrary, except the following: (c=center t=top b=bottom l=left r=right) USGS 1, 6b, 7tr.

Library of Congress Cataloging-in-Publication Data
Knapp, Dr. Brian J.
   Science Matters! / [Dr. Brian J. Knapp].
      p. cm.
   Includes index.
   Summary: Presents information on a wide variety of topics in basic biology, chemistry, and physics.
   Contents: v. 1. Food, teeth, and eating—v. 2. Helping plants grow well—v. 3. Properties of materials—v. 4. Rocks and soils—v. 5. Springs and magnets—v. 6. Light and shadows—v. 7. Moving and growing—v. 8. Habitats—v. 9. Keeping warm and cool—v. 10. Solids and liquids—v. 11. Friction—v. 12. Simple electricity—v. 13. Keeping healthy—v. 14. Life cycles—v. 15. Gases around us—v. 16. Changing from solids to liquids to gases—v. 17. Earth and beyond—v. 18. Changing sounds—v. 19. Adapting and surviving—v. 20. Microbes—v. 21. Dissolving—v. 22. Changing materials—v. 23. Forces in action—v. 24. How we see things—v. 25. Changing circuits.
   ISBN 0-7172-5834-3 (set)—ISBN 0-7172-5835-1 (v. 1)—ISBN 0-7172-5836-X (v. 2)—ISBN 0-7172-5837-8 (v. 3)—ISBN 0-7172-5838-6 (v. 4)—ISBN 0-7172-5839-4 (v. 5)—ISBN 0-7172-5840-8 (v. 6)—ISBN 0-7172-5841-6 (v. 7)—ISBN 0-7172-5842-4 (v. 8)—ISBN 0-7172-5843-2 (v. 9)—ISBN 0-7172-5844-0 (v. 10)—ISBN 0-7172-5845-9 (v. 11)—ISBN 0-7172-5846-7 (v. 12)—ISBN 0-7172-5847-5 (v. 13)—ISBN 0-7172-5848-3 (v. 14)—ISBN 0-7172-5849-1 (v. 15)—ISBN 0-7172-5850-5 (v. 16)—ISBN 0-7172-5851-3 (v. 17)—ISBN 0-7172-5852-1 (v. 18)—ISBN 0-7172-5853-X (v. 19)—ISBN 0-7172-5854-8 (v. 20)—ISBN 0-7172-5855-6 (v. 21)—ISBN 0-7172-5856-4 (v. 22)—ISBN 0-7172-5857-2 (v. 23)—ISBN 0-7172-5858-0 (v. 24)—ISBN 0-7172-5859-9 (v. 25)
   1. Science—Juvenile literature. [1. Science.] I. Title.

Q163.K48 2002
500—dc21
                                    2002017302